WATERLOO HIGH SCHOOL LIBRARY
1464 INDUSTRY RD.
ATWATER, OHIO 44201

GREAT MOMENTS IN

THE NBA CHAMPIONSHIPS

GREAT MOMENTS IN

THE NBA

CHAMPIONSHIPS

EDWARD F. DOLAN, JR.

FRANKLIN WATTS
New York / London / Toronto / Sydney / 1982
A TRIUMPH BOOK

796.32
DoL

Cover photo courtesy of Focus on Sports

Photographs courtesy of:
Naismith Memorial Basketball Hall of Fame: pp.
3, 4; United Press International: pp. 15, 26, 41, 45,
52, 59, 62, 69, 72, 77, 78.

Library of Congress Cataloging in Publication Data

Dolan, Edward F., 1924-
Great moments in the NBA championships.

(A Triumph book)
Includes index.
Summary: Traces the history of
professional basketball's championship playoffs
since the NBA's first season of 1949-50.
1. National Basketball Association—
History—Juvenile literature.
2. Basketball—Tournaments—United States—
History—Juvenile literature.
[1. National Basketball Association—History.
2. Basketball—History] I. Title. II. Title:
Great moments in the N.B.A. championships.
GV885.59.N37D64   796.32'3'0973   82-2046
ISBN 0-531-04406-8   AACR2

R. L. 2.7 Spache Revised Formula

Copyright © 1982 by Edward F. Dolan, Jr.
All rights reserved
Printed in the United States of America
5   4   3   2

CONTENTS

GREAT MOMENTS IN

THE NBA CHAMPIONSHIPS

CHAPTER 1

BIRTH OF A CHAMPIONSHIP

The year was 1891. The students at the small college in Springfield, Massachusetts, had a problem.

They played baseball in the spring. They played football in the autumn. But there was no indoor game for them during the winter. All they could do was exercise in the gymnasium. They found the exercises boring. And they let their physical education teacher know it.

His name was James A. Naismith. He tried having the students play soccer in the gym. But the place was too small. The ball smashed through several windows. Then he turned to rugby. The game is like football. It's full of rough tackling. There were many bruises and bumped heads when the players hit the floor.

Finally, Naismith tried lacrosse. It didn't work either. The players hit each other with the sticks.

Sometimes, the hits were accidental. Sometimes, they were on purpose.

A NEW GAME

Naismith knew that a brand-new game was needed. The teacher decided to invent a ball game that could be safely played indoors. Two teams would play. No bats or sticks would be used. The players wouldn't be allowed to hit each other.

They couldn't run with the ball. There would then be no tackling and bumped heads. Nor could the ball be kicked and sent whizzing through a window. It would be moved by bouncing it along off the floor. It could also be passed from one player to another. A fairly large ball would be needed for bouncing and passing. Naismith felt that a soccer ball would serve well.

Points would be scored by sending the ball into boxlike goals. Naismith set the goals high above the floor. This would force the players to hit them with arcing throws. Accuracy would be the skill needed. No one would be able to score by brute strength.

Naismith wrote thirteen rules for his new game. (Twelve of them are still used today.) Then he searched for two boxes for the goals. He found

*James A. Naismith invented
basketball in 1891*

*The first basketball games
were played with peach baskets.*

nothing suitable, and so he picked two peach baskets instead. He hung them 10 feet (3 m) above the floor at either end of the gym. Why 10 feet? Because he nailed the baskets to the gymnasium balcony. The balcony happened to be 10 feet high.

In December, 1891, the game was played for the first time. The students had a great time! They wanted to call the game "Naismith ball" in honor of their teacher. But he shook his head. He was a modest man. The name *basketball* was then chosen.

Basketball was invented at the International Young Men's Christian Association Training School. The school prepared men and women to help young people who came to YMCAs across the country. The school later became Springfield College.

THE GAME TAKES HOLD

In time, basketball became one of the most popular of games. First, it spread to YMCAs everywhere. Starting in 1895, it was taken up by high schools and colleges. It began to rival football and baseball as a school sport. By the 1920s and 1930s, such universities as Stanford, Holy Cross, and St. John's had famous basketball teams.

Even a high school — Passaic High in New Jersey — was known all across the country. Between 1919 and 1925, its team won 159 games in a row.

Finally, basketball moved to other countries. It became a part of the Olympic games. It developed into the worldwide sport that it is today.

But basketball did more than just grow. It also changed. The first games had nine players on each team. But there were too many people moving around the court. So the number was soon dropped to five. A larger ball replaced the soccer ball. It was the grandfather of today's basketball. Sometimes it was made of leather, and sometimes of rubber.

And the peach baskets were no longer used. They didn't look "official" enough for school games. They also caused a problem because they weren't open at the bottom. Someone had to climb a ladder and get the ball every time a goal was made. Metal hoops with a basketlike frame took their place.

The hoops were closed at the bottom. But each one had a chain. When the chain was pulled, the hoop tipped over, and the ball fell out. In 1906, someone finally invented a net basket with an open bottom.

THE PRO GAME

And there was yet another change. Basketball had started as an amateur sport. But soon a few players began to play for money. They formed teams and rented halls for their games. The spectators paid a small admission fee. Most of the money was used to pay the rent. The rest went to the players. Basketball had turned professional.

One of the first professional games was played at Trenton, New Jersey, in 1896. It was staged at the Masonic Hall and drew a large crowd. The money collected paid the rent. There was enough left over to give each player $15.

Soon, pro teams were playing in many eastern towns and cities. A professional league, the National Basketball League, was formed in 1898. Other leagues followed. The Central League was founded in western Pennsylvania in 1906. The New York State League took shape in 1911. The American Basketball League was formed in 1925.

The early professionals made some fine contributions to the game. For instance, there was coach Ed Wachter of the Troy Trojans in the New York State League. He didn't like the way the ball was passed from player to player. It was sent through the air and was easy to intercept. Ed developed the bounce pass. That made things tough for the opposition.

The coach also invented the fast break. Before, all the players had scrambled for the ball. But Ed set his men at strategic points on the floor. Then he sent two players after the ball. Whoever got the ball fired it over the defense to an unguarded teammate.

In many early basketball courts, the floor was surrounded by a chicken wire fence. The fence kept the ball from sailing into the audience. But the players looked as if they were inside a cage. And so they were called cagers. The nickname stuck.

The early days featured some excellent pro teams. One of the best was the Original Celtics of New York City. Between 1920 and 1928, the Celts won 720 out of 795 games. Two of their stars were Nat Holman and Joe Lapchick. Both went on to great careers in coaching.

But professional ball was slow to grow. Basketball was still young. It didn't attract as many fans as baseball and football. The crowds were usually small. One after another, the leagues folded.

Yet the professional game refused to die. It struggled on for years. A new National Basketball League (NBL) was started in 1937. Then, in 1946, the Basketball Association of America (BAA) came into being. It was formed by businessmen interested in pro basketball for two reasons.

First, they owned ice arenas in many cities and small towns. They wanted a game to bring people in when there were no ice hockey games. Second, they saw how popular school basketball had become. They were sure pro ball would thrill millions of fans.

Right off, the BAA got into a war with the NBL. Both leagues paid huge salaries to attract the top college stars. Each tried to steal the other's teams away. In 1948, the BAA took four of the NBL's best teams.

Both leagues were being hurt by the war. Both were spending more money than they could afford. Both were in danger of going out of business. There was only one way to end the war. In 1949 they merged into a single league — the National Basketball Association (NBA). Today, the NBA is *the* professional league in the United States.

The NBA started with seventeen teams. They were placed in three divisions — the Eastern, Western, and Central. The Eastern and Western Divisions were given six teams each. Five teams were placed in the Central Division. The divisions were set up as follows:

Eastern Division	*Western Division*
Baltimore Bullets	Anderson Packers
Boston Celtics	Denver Nuggets
New York Knickerbockers	Indianapolis Jets
Philadelphia Warriors	Sheboygan Redskins
Syracuse Nationals	Tri-Cities Blackhawks
Washington Capitols	Waterloo Hawks

Central Division

Chicago Stags
Fort Wayne Pistons
Minneapolis Lakers
Rochester Royals
St. Louis Bombers

The NBA had a rocky time in its first years. Pro ball was not yet widely popular. The 1949–50 season started with seventeen teams. The NBA dropped to eleven teams the next year. Many teams in the smaller cities didn't have the money to keep going. The league was down to eight teams by the 1957–58 season.

But finally pro ball caught on. More and more people came to the games each year. More and more cities wanted teams of their own. The NBA began to grow. By the 1980–81 season, it had twenty-three teams. They represented the largest cities. They played to packed houses. Countless fans watched the games on television. Professional basketball was a top American sport.

THE CHAMPIONSHIP

The NBA gives basketball fans an especially exciting event — the championship playoffs. At the end of each season, the top teams in each division play a series of games. There is an opening round, a semifinal round, and a championship round.

Two teams are left after the semifinal round. They square off in the finals and battle for the NBA championship. The winner is the number-one pro basketball outfit in the nation.

Every round is exciting. But the final round is the most exciting of all. The best players in the country are on the court. The national basketball crown is at stake. To win, a team must take four of seven games. The final round has given the sports world some of its greatest moments.

Let's relive the best of those moments.

CHAPTER 2

THE FIRST ONES

Minneapolis of the Central Division had been a top BAA team. The Lakers looked just as sharp in the NBA's first year, 1949–50. They posted a 51–17 record (51 wins, 17 losses) for the season. They headed for the playoffs.

Also headed for the playoffs were the Syracuse Nationals of the Eastern Division. Their season record was 51–13. They were to meet the Lakers head-on for the first NBA crown.

1949–50
MINNEAPOLIS LAKERS
vs.
SYRACUSE NATIONALS

The finest basketball player of the day led Minneapolis to the playoffs. George Mikan was a 6-foot

10-inch (2.08-m) center from DePaul University. George started his pro career with the Chicago Gears of the NBL in 1946. He moved to the Lakers in 1947.

In his first pro year, George averaged 21.3 points per game. The Mikan average jumped to 28.3 in the 1948–49 season. He scored 53 points in a game against the Baltimore Bullets. He dropped in more than 40 points in 7 games.

The new NBA saw him burn up the court in 1949–50. George scored 1,865 points for the season. He earned a 27.4 per-game average. Mikan led the league with the most field goals — 649. And the most foul shots — 567 of 728 tried. Playing against the Rochester Royals, he hit his season high — 51 points.

Working behind Mikan were stars Jim Pollard and Vern Mikkelsen. Fans said the three players were the best backboard men in the league.

Most sportswriters thought the Lakers would surely take the NBA's first title. And it certainly looked that way when the playoffs began. Minneapolis knocked off the Chicago Stags, the Fort Wayne Pistons, and the Anderson Packers. They had made it to the finals.

But the Syracuse Nationals also looked tough. They had defeated the mighty Philadelphia Warriors and the New York Knickerbockers.

The finals turned into a seesaw battle. After five games, Minneapolis led the series 3–2. Then came game 6. It was played in the Lakers' hometown. On hand was the biggest crowd ever to watch a pro game in Minneapolis. There were 9,812 fans in the stands. They were treated to a wild evening.

Both teams were charged up. The first period had plenty of action. A fight broke out between Jim Pollard and Syracuse guard Paul Seymour. Policemen had to break it up. Minutes later, Swede Carlson of the Lakers tussled with Billy Gabor. What about the second quarter? Gabor and Laker guard Slater Martin started swinging at each other!

Al Cervi, the Nationals' player-coach, livened up the third period. He became furious over an official's call. And he let the official know it in a loud and angry voice. He was thrown out of the game.

So, the fans saw a lot of fighting. And they saw some great basketball. Mikan was in top form. He hit 13 field goals and 14 foul shots. And he scored 40 points for the night. He was the game's leading scorer.

Minneapolis held a 51–39 lead at halftime. The Lakers stretched the lead to 81–56 in the third period. Syracuse closed the gap a little in the final frame. But the Nationals just couldn't catch up.

*George Mikan (dark uniform) led the
Minneapolis Lakers to the NBA crown
in the 1949–50 playoffs.*

With just 3 minutes left to play, the Lakers dropped in their 100th point. For the eighth time in the 1949–50 season, they hit the 100 mark. In the next minutes, they tallied another 10 points.

At the final buzzer, the score stood 110–95. The Lakers had taken the finals 4 games to 2. They owned the NBA's first championship crown.

George Mikan had put in one of his finest seasons as a pro. He would continue to play until the end of the 1953–54 season. He and the Lakers would win three more NBA crowns. Soon after George retired, he was given a great honor. An Associated Press poll named him the greatest basketball player of the first half of the twentieth century.

1950–51
ROCHESTER ROYALS
vs.
NEW YORK KNICKERBOCKERS

The NBA changed greatly after its first season. Six teams could not afford to stay in the league. They dropped out. The remaining eleven were placed in two divisions — the Eastern and the Western. The Central Division disappeared. The league now looked like this:

Eastern Division	Western Division
Baltimore Bullets	Fort Wayne Pistons
Boston Celtics	Indianapolis Olympians
New York Knickerbockers	Minneapolis Lakers
Philadelphia Warriors	Rochester Royals
Syracuse Nationals	Tri-Cities Blackhawks
Washington Capitols	

One team changed its name. Indianapolis had started out as the Jets. The team now became the Olympians.

The year 1950 was an important one for black players. Pro basketball had always been divided along color lines. Blacks and whites played in their own leagues. But now two black players joined the NBA. The New York Knicks hired Nat "Sweetwater" Clifton from the Harlem Globetrotters. The Boston Celtics drafted Chuck Cooper from Duquesne University in Pennsylvania. In the coming years, the finest black players in the country would enter the NBA.

The Rochester Royals and the New York Knicks made it to the finals in the 1950–51 playoffs. The Royals had a 41–27 record for the season. They made it to the finals by beating Fort Wayne and Minneapolis. The Knicks put in a 36–30 season.

In the playoffs, they downed Boston and Syracuse. A place in the finals was theirs.

Again, the finals proved to be a seesaw battle. The teams fought to a deadlock at 3 games apiece. Then came the seventh and deciding game. They gave the NBA championships one of the most hair-raising finishes ever.

The seventh game was played at Rochester. The Royals held a 14-point lead at halftime. But New York slowly caught up in the next frames. The Knicks inched into a 74–72 lead. There were just 2 minutes left to play. The Royals bounced right back and went ahead 75–74. Then it was New York's turn. The Knicks dropped in a foul shot. The score was tied at 75–75.

Just 59 seconds remained to the final buzzer. Guard Bob Davies of Rochester took the ball. He moved into position for a short-range layup. The Knicks' Dick Maguire came at him. Dick had to stop the shot. It could win the game. But he charged too hard. The referee's whistle screamed. Maguire was called for a foul. Two free throws went to Davies and the Royals.

Davies took his place at the foul line. The arena became silent as the fans held their breath. Bob sent the ball in an arc. It dropped through the hoop. The score changed to 76–75.

There was a wild cheer. Then the crowd again held its breath. Bob's face was a mask of concentration. He released the ball. It sailed to the basket — and dropped in on target! Rochester's lead went up another notch, to 77–75.

The arena shook with the thunder of the crowd. Less than 30 seconds remained. Desperately, the Knicks tried for a goal. But Rochester's Red Holzman got the ball. He fired a bullet pass to teammate Jack Coleman. Coleman raced for the basket and curled in a shot.

The score jumped to 79–75. Seconds later, the final buzzer sounded.

That last basket had been a great one. But it hadn't been necessary. Bob Davies' two foul shots had given the Royals the win and the NBA crown.

The championship was an important one for the Rochester Royals. It was to be their only NBA crown. They would continue to play in Rochester until 1957. Then they would move and become the Cincinnati Royals.

The Lakers were the playoff stars after Rochester's win. Starting in 1951–52, Minneapolis took the crown three years in a row.

While the Lakers were winning, another team was suffering bad luck in the playoffs. The Boston

Celtics were wiped out in either the opening round or the semifinals. At last, in 1956–57, they grabbed the championship. They beat the St. Louis Hawks. They came close to winning the next year. But this time, the Hawks beat them.

The Hawks had started in the NBA as the Tri-Cities Blackhawks. They moved to Milwaukee in the early 1950s. Then they went to St. Louis in 1955. They later became the Atlanta Hawks.

The Celts' luck changed in the 1958–59 season. They were about to set an NBA record. They would take the pro crown eight times in a row! It's a record that's never been broken.

CHAPTER 3

THE CELTIC YEARS

The Boston Celtics were formed in 1946. At first, they lost most games. The Celts' record for the 1946–47 season was a sad 22–38. It was even sadder in 1949–50 when it stood at 22–46.

But, starting in 1950, some fine people came to the Celtics. First, Arnold "Red" Auerbach became the coach. Auerbach was a tough leader. He'd been a star at George Washington University in Washington, D.C. Then, he had coached the Syracuse Nationals and the Tri-Cities Blackhawks. He would turn Boston into an all-time winner.

In 1950, a young backcourtman joined the Celtics. He was from Holy Cross College. His name was Bob Cousy. At first, Auerbach didn't think much of Cousy. Bob stood just an inch (2.5 cm) over 6 feet (1.8 m) tall. The coach felt he was too short for the pro game.

But Bob proved him wrong. He became a Celtic star. In fact, he became one of the top players in the NBA. In his rookie year, Bob ranked ninth in scoring in the league. He was second in assists in the following year, with 441. Then he led the league in assists for eight straight years. Right from the start, he was known as "Cooz." Then, he earned the nicknames "Mr. Basketball" and "the Mighty Midget."

Bob's playing style brought many new fans to the Boston games. He was a master at faking and palming the ball. And his dribbling was really something to see. Cooz not only dribbled the ball to his front. He could dribble behind his back!

Bob said he'd invented his behind-the-back dribble at Holy Cross. In a game against Loyola, he had tried to get around an opponent. To do so, he had to shift the ball from one hand to another. But the Loyola man had him too well guarded. Bob couldn't make the shift in front of his body. So, he sent the ball behind his back.

Auerbach and Cousy helped Boston take second place in the Eastern Division in 1950. Then, for several years, the Celts were always in the second or third spot. They constantly earned a place in the playoffs. But bad luck dogged them. They never made it to the finals.

Then the team took on more fine players. One was Tom Heinsohn, a forward from Holy Cross. He won Rookie of the Year honors in 1956–57. Another was guard Bill Sharman. He became known as the best foul shooter in the league. In 1956–57, Bill set an NBA record with 56 foul shots in a row.

Then came Bill Russell from the University of San Francisco. Standing 6 feet 10 inches (2.08 m), Bill has been called the best defensive man ever to play basketball. He outdid himself in one of his first games against the Philadelphia Warriors. He held his man scoreless for 38 minutes.

By 1956–57, Boston was a powerhouse team. The Celts posted a 44–28 record. They took first place in the Eastern Division. On to the playoffs they went. This time, nothing could stop them from reaching the finals.

1956–57
BOSTON CELTICS
vs.
ST. LOUIS HAWKS

The Celts beat Syracuse 3–0 in the semifinals. Pitted against them for the crown were the St. Louis Hawks. The Hawks also had come through the semifinals without a loss. They'd dusted off Minneapolis.

Pro basketball had been catching on everywhere because of Bob Cousy's playing. The playoffs had always attracted crowds from the East and Midwest. But now the whole country was watching. For the first time, the playoffs had become a truly national event.

Boston and St. Louis gave the country a good series. They battled for 6 games. Each team won 3 games.

The seventh game was played at Boston Garden. Packed into the place were 13,909 fans. They were treated to a thrilling finish.

Boston led 83–77 as the fourth quarter opened. Bob Cousy set up the first score of the period. He neatly fed the ball to a teammate for a basket. But the Hawks replied with 9 points in a row. They took the lead. Then, with just 20 seconds left, Bill Russell hit on a pivot. The Celts were in front again. Cousy added another point with a foul shot. Boston held a slim 103–101 edge.

Jack Coleman of St. Louis tried to close the gap. He fired a beautiful shot. But Bill Russell jumped high and blocked the ball. The clock was down to 6 seconds. Could Boston hold on? They were so close to their first NBA crown. But Russell fouled

Bob Pettit. The Hawks' star took two free throws. Both dropped in. The final buzzer sounded. The score stood at 103–103. The game went into overtime.

The score moved to 111–111 in the overtime period. The teams kept trading points until only 15 seconds remained. Tommy Heinsohn swept in under the basket for a layup. It put Boston ahead 113–111. Again the Celts seemed ready to take the crown. If only they could hold on!

But they couldn't. The Hawks' Jack Coleman let fly with a one-handed shot. The ball thumped into the basket. Things were even again! Another one-hander, by Boston's Bill Sharman, came a few seconds later. This time, the ball hit the rim. The score was still holding at 113–113 when the period ended.

What a game! The fans were hoarse from cheering. But they kept up their thunder during the second overtime period. Both teams scored right away. Next, Bill Russell gave Boston 2 points with a fine layup. Then Tom Heinsohn dropped in a long shot. The Celts led 121–120.

St. Louis put the game into yet another tie — 121–121 — with a foul shot. Boston's Frank Ramsey quickly grabbed the lead back. After being fouled, he hit one of two free throws. Then he let

*Boston's Bob Cousy leaps high and palms
the ball to teammate Tom Heinsohn
during the 1956–57 championship battle.*

loose with a long one-hander. The Celts went to the front, 124–121.

But the Hawks weren't finished yet. They closed things to 124–123 with two foul shots. Just 23 seconds remained. Alex Hannum of St. Louis had the ball. He was called for walking. The ball went to Boston. The clock ticked down to 12 seconds. Then Hannum fouled Jim Loscutoff. The Boston guard dropped in a 1-pointer. It moved the score to 125–123.

Only 1 second remained. Hawk Alex Hannum took the ball. He pegged a long shot to the backboard. The ball traveled the length of the court. A gasp went through the arena. His teammate, Bob Pettit, raced to the basket. Bob was to take the ball as it bounced off the backboard. It was a trick play the Hawks had practiced all season long. It looked like a sure tally that would tie the score again. The crowd held its breath. Bob took the shot. He sent the ball to the basket. . . .

And then the Boston fans were screaming in glee.

The ball had hit the rim! It bounced away!

The game was over. The Celts had the win — and their first NBA crown.

Boston returned to the playoffs in 1957–58. Again, the Celts reached the finals. Again, they faced the Hawks. This time, the crown went to St. Louis 4–2.

Then the 1958–59 playoffs rolled around. Boston moved into the finals after downing Syracuse in the semifinals. The Celts were about to make basketball history. They were about to take eight championships in a row.

1958–59
BOSTON CELTICS
vs.
MINNEAPOLIS LAKERS

Boston faced the Minneapolis Lakers in the championship round. The Lakers had looked good in the semifinals. They had beaten a tough St. Louis squad. But they were no match for the Celts. Boston took the first 3 games.

Game 4 was tougher for the Celts. They led by just 1 point when the final period opened. Then Elgin Baylor and Bob Leonard pushed the Lakers ahead. The Celts fought back. They regained the front spot. They slowly widened the gap. With just seconds left to go, they brought Frank Ramsey down under the basket. He hit a perfect layup. It put the game out of reach for the Lakers. The final score was 118–113 for Boston.

The win was a sweet one for the Celts. It gave them their second NBA crown. And they were the first team ever to take the championship round in a 4–0 clean sweep.

They were happy for another reason. The win made up for the way Minneapolis's Elgin Baylor had treated them one night during the regular season. The big forward had tagged them for 64 points. Elgin was now in his second year with the Lakers. He was to have an outstanding pro career. Before he was done, he would score 23,149 points.

The next two years saw the Celts play St. Louis in the finals. They won by a slim 4–3 margin in 1959–60. The 1960–61 margin was wide — 4–1. The Celts now had their fourth NBA crown. It was their third crown in a row.

1961–62
BOSTON CELTICS
vs.
LOS ANGELES LAKERS

Once again, Boston met the Lakers in the finals. This time, the Lakers were playing for Los Angeles. They had moved to California at the start of the season. The Lakers defeated St. Louis in semifinal play. Boston downed the Cincinnati Royals.

The championship series stood at 3–3 after 6 games. As the fourth quarter opened in game 7, the score was tied 75–75. The teams moved up and down the court, fighting hard. It was a fight that Boston seemed to be winning. The Celts forged ahead 100–96. There was just over a minute to go.

Then L.A.'s Frank Selvy took over. He dropped in a toss at the 40-second mark. The gap closed to 100–98. With 20 seconds left, he hit again for a 100–100 tie. Finally, in the last 3 seconds, Frank unleashed another shot. The ball seemed about to drop in. But it hit the rim. The buzzer sounded.

It seemed to be 1956–57 all over again. Here was another overtime battle.

Elgin Baylor put the Lakers ahead. He sank two free throws early in the overtime period. Bill Russell tied the score with a shot. Then his teammate Sam Jones tallied. Boston moved ahead 104–102. Sam was fouled on the play. He took a free throw. It was good. Up went the score to 105–102.

Russell moved things to 107–102 on two foul shots. Bob Cousy and the Lakers' Frank Selvy each took a free throw. Now the score was 108–103. Next, Sam Jones sent in a long rocket. Boston jumped to a 110–103 lead. Then the Lakers' Tom Hawkins got hot. He dropped in two tosses. The score closed to 110–107.

And that's where it stayed. Bob Cousy took the ball and dribbled the last seconds away.

The Celts now had five NBA crowns. They had taken four in a row. It was a sensational record. But the Boston team wasn't finished yet.

In the 1962–63 finals, the Celts met Los Angeles again. This time, they took the championship 4–2.

The series marked the close of Bob Cousy's pro career. He had been a player for thirteen years. He held a lifetime record of 6,959 assists and 16,960 points. Bob went on to become a fine coach, first at Boston College and then with the Cincinnati Royals. He was named to basketball's Hall of Fame in 1970.

Boston faced another California team when the 1963–64 finals came up — the San Francisco Warriors. They had started life in 1947 as the Philadelphia Warriors. They moved west in 1963. The Celts knocked them off 4–1. The Boston crew now had seven NBA crowns. They'd taken six in a row.

The Celtics took their seventh straight title in 1964–65. They met their old foe, the Lakers, and downed them 4–1. Boston won the final game by a whopping 129–96 margin.

But it looked as if there might be trouble at the end of the next season.

1965–66
BOSTON CELTICS
vs.
LOS ANGELES LAKERS

For ten years, the Celtics had placed first in the Eastern Division. This time, they came in second behind the Philadelphia 76ers. The 76ers were the old Syracuse Nationals. They had moved to Philadelphia in 1964. Now they were led by the great Wilt Chamberlain.

But the Celts knocked over Wilt's crew in the semifinals of the playoffs. Once again, they moved to the finals. And, once again, they fought the Lakers.

At first, the Celts looked strong. They jumped to a 3–1 lead in the series. But the Lakers came charging back. They took 2 games in a row to tie things 3–3. Sloppy play by Boston helped L.A. to the two wins.

But the Celts cleaned up their act for game 7 in Boston. They featured fast breaks and hard defensive play. The Celts forged ahead 27–20 in the first period. They stayed in the lead for the rest of the game.

Bill Russell scored 25 points and nailed down 32 rebounds. Sam Jones scored 22. John Havlicek posted 16. John had joined the Celts in 1962. He did double duty as a guard and forward. Known as Hondo, he was on his way to becoming a great NBA star. He would soon captain the Celts.

And Boston's excellent defensive play bottled up the Lakers' Elgin Baylor. The Celts held him to only 2 points in the first half. Elgin finished the night with 18 points.

Only his teammate Jerry West seemed able to get through the Boston defense. The fast-moving guard tallied 36 points. He became the game's highest scorer. Jerry had been with the Lakers since 1960. Already, he was considered one of the finest guards in the business. He would play until 1974. Then he would coach the Lakers.

By the third quarter, the Celts held a 19-point lead. Desperately, the Lakers tried to catch up in the final period. They came close — but not close enough. Coach Red Auerbach's eyes were on Celt Sam Jones. Sam sank a shot from 35 feet (10.5 m) away in the last seconds. The coach took out a cigar and lighted it. Red always smoked a cigar when victory was at hand. He knew that his Celts had a lock on the crown.

He was right. The score stood 95–92 for Boston at the final buzzer.

The win was a special one for Auerbach. He planned to retire at the end of the series. His team had given him the NBA title as a going-away present. As a pro coach, Red had 1,037 wins to his credit. He had turned Boston into an all-time winner. Red became the club's general manager. He made his way to the Hall of Fame in 1968.

Bill Russell became the Celts' coach when Red left. Bill was the first black man ever to coach a major American sports team.

Boston's winning streak couldn't last forever. In the 1966–67 season, the Celts again placed second to Philadelphia in the Eastern Division. They met the 76ers in the semifinals and were downed 4–1. Philadelphia and Wilt Chamberlain then took the crown. They defeated San Francisco 4–2 in the championship round.

But the Celts bounced back in the next years. Twice, they beat the Lakers for the crown — in 1967–68 and 1968–69. In 1973–74, they picked up another championship by beating the Milwaukee Bucks. Still another crown was theirs in 1975–76. They beat the Phoenix Suns. And there was still another one to come. They won a 4–2 battle with the Houston Rockets in 1980–81.

The Celts have won fourteen championships over the years. And, they've taken eight straight crowns. Those records seem unbeatable. They'll stand for a long time to come in pro basketball. Perhaps they'll stand forever!

CHAPTER
4

A GREAT SEASON
FOR THE KNICKS

A lot was happening in the NBA while the Celtics were winning their championships.

The league grew. There were only eight NBA teams when the Celtics began their winning streak. By 1967 there were twelve. During the 1968–69 season, the NBA expanded to fourteen.

Each division now boasted seven teams. The league looked like this:

Eastern Division	*Western Division*
Baltimore Bullets	Atlanta Hawks
Boston Celtics	Chicago Bulls
Cincinnati Royals	Los Angeles Lakers
Detroit Pistons	Phoenix Suns
Milwaukee Bucks	San Diego Rockets
New York Knickerbockers	San Francisco Warriors
Philadelphia 76ers	Seattle Super Sonics

Several teams had changed cities. The Lakers and Warriors went to California. The Syracuse Nationals headed for Philadelphia. They changed their name to the 76ers. The Hawks left St. Louis and settled in Atlanta. The Fort Wayne Pistons chose Detroit as their new home.

Fourteen teams were now playing. The competition was tougher than ever. But one of the oldest teams in pro basketball would take the 1969–70 crown. That team was the New York Knickerbockers. Along with the Celtics and the Warriors, the Knicks had been formed in 1946.

THE KNICKS

The Knicks were a powerhouse team in the early 1950s. They came close to the NBA title in 1950–51. But they lost the playoff finals to Rochester 4–3.

In the next two seasons, they took first place in the Eastern Division. Both times, the New Yorkers couldn't make it through the playoffs.

Then the team started to slide downhill. It slipped into second place in the East in 1954–55. After that, it hit the cellar. And there — except for the 1958–59 season — the Knicks stayed for ten long years.

No one likes the cellar. And so the Knicks brought in fine new talent in the early 1960s. Grambling's Willis Reed and that great ball thief, Walt Frazier, came. The 6-foot 10-inch (2.08-m) Reed was so inspiring, he soon became the team captain. By 1964–65, he was ranked among the NBA's top rebounders. He tallied 1,175 rebounds that season, averaging 14.7 per game. As for Walt, he moved up among the league's top men in assists. He posted 635 in 1968–69.

The Knicks started to climb out of the cellar in 1966–67. They moved into the second-from-last place in the East. The next two years saw them in third place.

The Knicks looked better than ever as the 1969–70 season opened. They had Reed at center and Frazier at guard. The team boasted such stars as Dave DeBusschere, Bill Bradley, and Dick Barnett. DeBusschere was a fine forward. Bradley made great jump shots. Barnett was a master of long ones.

Under Coach Red Holzman, the Knicks won 17 of their first 18 games. Reporters called it the best start ever seen in the NBA.

Then the New Yorkers set a league record that left everyone gasping. They won their next 18 games in a row!

A WILD FINISH

Their final win in that string of 18 came in late November, 1969. It had a wild finish. With just 16 seconds left to play, the Knicks were trailing the Cincinnati Royals by 5 points. Then came some blinding action.

First, Reed was fouled by Tom Van Arsdale and took two free throws. He sank them both. Then a pass went to Van Arsdale at midcourt. But Dave DeBusschere intercepted. He drove in under the basket for a perfect layup. Finally, Walt Frazier was fouled as he tried a jump shot that missed. He was given two free throws. Both dropped through the hoop.

The Knicks had scored 6 points in 16 seconds. When the final buzzer sounded, they owned a 106–105 win.

The New Yorkers rolled through the rest of the year. They ended the season with a 60–22 record. They were on top in the East.

Into the playoffs they went. In the first round, the Knicks downed Baltimore. The semifinals matched them with Milwaukee. They took care of the Bucks, though they were up against an amazing young rookie named Lew Alcindor. Everyone knew he was headed for greatness. One day, he would change his name to Kareem Abdul-Jabbar.

The Knicks were to play the Los Angeles Lakers in the championship. Wilt Chamberlain was now with the L.A. squad. They had come through the season with a 46–36 record. To get into the finals, they had defeated Phoenix and Atlanta.

1969–70
NEW YORK KNICKS
vs.
LOS ANGELES LAKERS

The championship round opened with 2 games at Madison Square Garden in New York City. Each team took a win. The scoring honors in both games went to Jerry West of the Lakers. He dropped in 33 points and then 34.

Games 3 and 4 were played at Los Angeles. Again, each team won. The Knicks nailed down game 3 in overtime. Jerry West caused the overtime. His team was trailing in the final seconds of regulation play. But he let fly with a field goal just as the buzzer sounded. It was quite a toss. The ball arced 55 feet (16.5 m) into the basket to tie things up.

The series returned to New York for game 5. At this point, the Knicks ran into some bad luck. Willis Reed took a spill in the first half. He limped from the court. A muscle in his hip was torn. He was finished for the night — perhaps even for the rest of the series.

The New York fans were worried. Their team had lost its captain, its top scorer, and its top rebounder. Also, Willis had been doing a great job guarding Wilt Chamberlain. Everyone was sure Wilt would run wild. The game looked to be a sure win for the Lakers. They jumped to a 13-point lead by halftime.

But the Knicks came out in the second half with a 1–3–1 offense. It put Bill Bradley in the middle. Walt Frazier worked the top of the key. Cazzie Russell and Dick Barnett were out on the wings. Dave DeBusschere took care of the baseline. They launched an attack that made hash out of the Lakers' tight defense.

And the New Yorkers looked just as good on defense. They concentrated on keeping Chamberlain away from the basket. Wherever he turned,

The Knicks' Willis Reed
leaps high as he and
Happy Hairston of the Lakers
go after the ball during
1969–70 playoff action.

· 40 ·

Wilt found the passing lanes to him closed off. On top of all else, the Knicks constantly stole the ball. By himself, Walt Frazier made three steals in the final 12 minutes of play.

The result: the Knicks led the series 3–2 at game's end. They needed just one more win to take the crown. Despite the great performance, their fans were still worried. How long would Willis Reed's injury keep him out of action? That final win would be hard to get without Reed. Wilt Chamberlain would see to *that*.

Men shorter than Wilt had managed to control him for one game. But they couldn't keep it up for the rest of the series. Only Willis Reed could do it. He had plenty of strength and experience. It made up for the 4 inches (10 cm) of height that he lacked on Chamberlain.

Game 6 was played in Los Angeles. Limping and in obvious pain, Willis was sidelined. And Chamberlain got back at the New York defense for the way they'd handled him in the fifth game. No one could hold the 7-foot (1.82-m) giant back. Charging hard, he scored 45 points and pulled in 27 rebounds. Jerry West came right behind him with 33 points and 13 assists. The Lakers ran away with the game. They won by a margin of 22 points. The series was tied at 3–3.

Now, the New York fans were really worried. The series returned to New York for the seventh and deciding game. That terrible question remained. Would Willis be able to play? Without him, the title seemed as good as lost.

The Final Game

There were 19,500 people on hand for the action. No word had yet come through on Reed. The Knicks took to the court for their warm-up practice. Reed was nowhere in sight. The fans groaned. Then they cheered. Another player was coming out. The cheer died. The late arrival was Cazzie Russell.

At that moment, Willis was in the dressing room. He was in uniform. He'd been examined by a doctor and had received a pain-killing shot. He said that he felt ready to play.

Coach Red Holzman nodded. Willis trotted out to the court. A roar shook the arena. It continued as he tried a few practice shots. The mighty leader of the Knicks would be in the game! Wilt Chamberlain faced a tough man. The title wasn't as good as lost after all.

The game started. Just 18 seconds later, Willis tried his first shot. The arena seemed to shake with the thunder of the crowd. The ball dropped in on target. One minute later, Willis let loose with another shot. In it sailed, giving the Knicks a 5–2 lead.

Actually, those were the only baskets Reed made in the game. The big center couldn't move fast enough or jump well enough to score. He was limping. Even with the pain-killing shots, he was hurting. He moved more and more slowly as the evening wore on.

But his lack of scoring didn't matter. What mattered was that he did a fine job of guarding Chamberlain. Time and again, he bottled Chamberlain up. Wilt couldn't run wild.

And there was something else even more important. Reed inspired his teammates. The Knicks believed in teamwork — especially when the going was tough. Now they saw Willis giving everything he had. They came together and played better than ever. They seemed to be telling Willis, "Don't worry if you can't score. We'll take care of things for you."

And they did. The New Yorkers posted 38 points in the first quarter. They held Los Angeles to 24. Then, in the second period, they ran the score up to 69–42. They held a whopping 27-point lead.

Two stars go against each other in the 1969–70 final round: Jerry West of the Lakers tries to dribble past New York's Walt Frazier.

There were some tense minutes in the third quarter. The Knicks started to miss all their shots. The Lakers tried to take advantage of the situation. They launched a hard attack. But the New Yorkers recovered. They knocked the attack back fast. The Knicks surged far ahead — and stayed ahead for the rest of the game.

Not only did the Knicks work well as a team. They also put in some great individual performances. Reporters said Walt Frazier played the finest game of his career. Never letting down once, Walt led the team with 36 points. He posted 19 assists and took 7 rebounds. And he stole the ball five times. The best Lakers — Chamberlain, Jerry West, and Elgin Baylor — were among his victims.

Dick Barnett contributed 21 points to New York's cause. Bill Bradley scored 17 points and made 5 assists. Dave DeBusschere dropped in 18 points. He was the rebounding star of the night. He took 17 rebounds.

All the teamwork and individual effort could end in just one way. The Knicks owned the NBA crown when the final buzzer sounded. The scoreboard showed that they had a 113–99 win.

At last! They'd spent years in the cellar. And now New York had claimed its first NBA championship. It was an accomplishment that the team and New York City would never forget.

Three of the biggest sports crowns in the country had come to New York in just sixteen months. The New York Jets, led by quarterback Joe Namath, had won the Super Bowl in January, 1969. In October, the "amazing" Mets had won the World Series after years of being the most laughed-at team in baseball. And now the Knicks had the NBA championship.

But there was more to come from the Knicks. They were to bring the title home again. The next time would be at the end of the 1972–73 season. Their victim would again be the Lakers. New York would take the final game 102–93. They would claim the series 4–1.

CHAPTER 5

RECORD SETTERS

Pro basketball was more popular than ever by the 1970–71 season. Three more teams joined the NBA. They brought the number of teams up to seventeen.

The league was now quite large. It had to be divided into conferences and divisions. There were two conferences — the Eastern and Western. Each conference contained two divisions.

The NBA now shaped up like this:

EASTERN CONFERENCE	WESTERN CONFERENCE
Atlantic Division	*Midwest Division*
Boston Celtics	Chicago Bulls
Buffalo Braves	Detroit Pistons
New York Knickerbockers	Milwaukee Bucks
Philadelphia 76ers	Phoenix Suns

Central Division	*Pacific Division*
Atlanta Hawks	Los Angeles Lakers
Baltimore Bullets	Portland Trail Blazers
Cincinnati Royals	San Diego Rockets
Cleveland Cavaliers	San Francisco Warriers
	Seattle Super Sonics

The 1970s brought even more changes in the NBA. In 1971, the San Francisco club changed its name to the Golden State Warriors. The Rockets left San Diego. They moved to Houston, Texas. The Buffalo Braves later replaced them in San Diego and became the Clippers. The Cincinnati Royals shifted to Kansas City. They took a new name, the Kings.

And, the NBA saw some great playoff action in the 1970s. Two teams matched an old playoff record. One team posted the best seasonal record ever in the league.

1970–71
MILWAUKEE BUCKS
vs.
BALTIMORE BULLETS

The Milwaukee Bucks ranked among the newest teams in the NBA. It had been formed in the 1968 expansion. The club's first season was a disaster. Milwaukee ended with a 27–55 record. They placed last in the Eastern Division.

But the bad season was a blessing in disguise. They were the cellar team. So the Bucks got a high pick in the 1969 college draft. They chose a 7-foot 1-inch (2.15-m) star from UCLA. His name was Lew Alcindor.

Right off, Lew burned up the NBA courts. He took Rookie of the Year honors by scoring 2,361 points. His deadly aim gave him a per-game average of 28.8. It made him the second highest scorer in the NBA for 1969–70. He was right behind Jerry West of the Lakers. As a result, the Bucks landed in second place in the Midwest Division. Their seasonal record stood at 58–26.

It was quite a change for Milwaukee. The club headed for the playoffs. But they lost to the Knicks in the semifinals. New York took the NBA championship by downing the Lakers 4–3.

In 1970, the Bucks got another great player — the veteran Oscar Robertson. Oscar had been a star with the Cincinnati Royals. He was one of the finest playmakers in the game. During his career, he would set a league record for assists. He posted 9,887. Twice in the 1960s, Robertson led the NBA in free-throw accuracy.

Lew and Oscar worked beautifully together. Lew became known as Mr. Inside. Oscar was dubbed Mr. Outside. They led the Bucks to a sensational 1970–71 season. The team took 66 wins against 16 losses. Milwaukee topped New York's old record of 18 straight wins. The Bucks nailed down 20 in a row!

At season's end, the Bucks ranked first in the Midwest Division. They moved into the playoffs. They knocked off San Francisco in the opening round. Then they put the Lakers away in the semifinals.

The Bucks went against Baltimore in the finals. They proved too strong for the Bullets. They won the games by margins of 10, 19, 8, and 12 points. The NBA championship was theirs, 4–0. They'd done what Boston had done to the Lakers in the 1958–59 finals. Milwaukee became the second NBA team to take the crown with a clean sweep. And it was the first expansion team to win the championship.

Alcindor and Robertson performed like clockwork in the finals. In the last game, Lew tallied 27 points. His average for the previous three games also was 27. One year later, Lew joined the Islam religion. He became a Muslim and changed his name to Kareem Abdul-Jabbar.

*Lew Alcindor (33) (Kareem Abdul-Jabbar)
of the Milwaukee Bucks grabs the ball under
Baltimore's basket during the 1970–71
playoff finals. Teammate Bob Dandridge
keeps the Bullets' Jack Marin away.*

Oscar was high man in the last game with 30 points. He hit 11 of 15 field goals and had 9 assists. The game was his 886th for the NBA.

1971–72
LOS ANGELES LAKERS
vs.
NEW YORK KNICKERBOCKERS

1971–72 would be a season of sweet revenge for the Lakers. They had won four championships in their first NBA years as the Minneapolis Lakers. (And they'd won one while in the BAA.) But then they had lost the crown seven times to the Celtics and once to the Knicks.

This year, nothing was to stop them from taking the championship round.

Led by Wilt Chamberlain and Jerry West, the Lakers came to the playoffs after setting three records. First, they posted 69 wins and only 13 losses for the season. No team had ever won *that* many games in a season.

Second, they set a new record for straight-game victories. The Bucks had broken the Knicks' record. Now the Lakers completely blasted the Milwaukee record. They took an amazing 33 games in a row!

Finally, Wilt Chamberlain set a record for career scoring. It happened in a game against the Phoenix Suns in February 1972. He dropped in his 30,000th regular-season point. Wilt would continue to play until the end of the 1972–73 season. His career total would be tops in the NBA — 31,419.

The Lakers looked unbeatable when they came to the playoffs. They dusted off the Chicago Bulls in the opening round. Next, they took care of the Bucks in the semifinals. Then they leaped ahead of the New York Knicks 3–1 in the finals.

But in game 5, the Lakers faced a very tough New York crew. They led by only 1 point at the end of the first period. The game was tied at the half. Things stood at 83–80 for Los Angeles as the final period opened. Then the Lakers took charge. They outrebounded the Knicks. They hit them hard offensively. They smothered them defensively. And they surged to a 114–110 win.

After all the years of losing the finals, the Lakers had the NBA crown again.

The night was a great one for West and Chamberlain. Jerry socked away 33 points. Chamberlain tallied 24 points, grabbed 29 rebounds, and played 46 minutes. He did all this with a sprained wrist that was heavily taped!

The Lakers enjoyed their revenge. They wanted more when they met the Knicks again. It was at the end of the 1972–73 season. But the Knicks came out ahead, 4–1.

1974–75
GOLDEN STATE WARRIORS
vs.
WASHINGTON BULLETS

In 1973, the Baltimore Bullets moved to a new city. They went to Washington, D.C., and changed their name. For one season, they played as the Capital Bullets. Then they decided to call themselves the Washington Bullets.

The 1974–75 season proved to be one of their best. The Bullets topped the Central Division with a 60–22 record. In the opening round of the playoffs, they defeated the Buffalo Braves. The semifinals saw them drop Boston. They moved into the finals to face the Golden State Warriors.

Golden State had placed first in the Pacific Division. The Warriors reached the finals by edging past the Chicago Bulls in semifinal play. They had beaten the Seattle Super Sonics in the opening round.

Basketball fans were surprised to see Golden

State do well in the playoffs. Golden State came from the league's weakest division. They were now up against some pretty tough competition. Further, the team itself didn't look too strong. Yes, the Warriors had fine players. But the lineup was short of superstars. There was just one on the squad — the 6-foot 7-inch (2-m) Rick Barry. So, the Warriors should have been knocked out early in the playoffs. Everyone said so.

But Golden State seemed to get better and better with each playoff game. The Warriors played a solid, fundamental game. Their teamwork was fine. And coach Al Attles handled his men in a special way. He used many substitutions. Every player worked only a few minutes in each game. This kept the regulars fresh and rested. Only Rick Barry played for 40 minutes or more per game.

Rick was one of the finest performers in pro ball. He had joined the Warriors in 1965 from the University of Miami. In his second year, he beat out Wilt Chamberlain and Oscar Robertson as the league's top scorer. Rick tallied 2,775 points for a per-game average of 35.6. He led the Warriors to the NBA finals in 1966–67. They lost 4–2 to Philadelphia.

In 1967, Rick left Golden State. He went to the new American Basketball Association. He played in the ABA for the Oakland Oaks and the New York Nets. Rick starred for both teams. He and the Nets won the ABA crown in 1969.

Rick returned to the Warriors in 1972. And now here he was in the 1974–75 playoffs.

The fans were still certain that the Warriors had no chance for the title. The Bullets seemed to be a much stronger team. They boasted such stars as Elvin Hayes, Wes Unseld, Kevin Porter, and Phil Chenier. Golden State was sure to lose.

For a time in game 1, the fans seemed to be right. The Bullets jumped to an early lead. It was a big one. But the Warriors came clawing back. They pulled a narrow victory out of the hat. Then they won game 2 by the narrowest margin possible — 1 point. Finally, after trailing much of the time, they took game 3.

The fans were amazed. The Warriors were supposed to lose. Instead, they held a 3–0 lead. They were on the brink of taking the series. Could they now match a record set by the Celts and the Bucks? Could they become the third team in NBA history to win the crown with a clean sweep?

The fans didn't think so. The Bullets might not take the crown. No team had ever come from 3 games behind to win the championship. But they wouldn't stand still for a clean sweep. They were too strong for *that*. They'd stage a comeback in game 4.

A comeback looked like a sure thing at the start of the game. The Bullets jumped to a 10–4 lead. Then they moved even farther ahead, thanks mainly to guard Kevin Porter. He kept slipping past the Warrior defense and sinking baskets. The first period ended with Washington out front 36–22. The Bullets had a 14-point lead. The fans thought Golden State could kiss a clean sweep goodbye.

But then the Warriors began to click. Led by Barry, they hit 67 percent of their shots. They trailed by only 5 points — 52–48 — at halftime.

Rick and his teammates continued to close the gap in the third quarter. Late in the period, the Warriors finally took the lead. Phil Smith hit a jumper. It put Golden State ahead by 1 point — 66–65.

Golden State Warrior Keith (Jamaal) Wilkes takes a rebound in the 1974–75 finals. Behind him is Phil Chenier of the Washington Bullets.

Now it was Washington's turn to fight back. The Bullets recaptured the lead. They held a 73–70 edge as the fourth period opened. The teams battled hard. Each scored on good shots. But the Bullets widened the gap as the minutes passed. With just under 5 minutes left, Washington's Elvin Hayes connected with a jumper. The score stood at 92–84 for the Bullets.

The Bullets had an 8-point edge. There could be no doubt about it this time. Washington had put a lock on the game. No clean sweep for the Warriors.

But no! Once more, Rick and the Warriors began to click. They closed to 92–88. Then rookie Keith Wilkes (he soon changed his first name to Jamaal) tried a jump shot. It was good. Next, Wilkes leaped high for a Warrior rebound. He reached across Wes Unseld to get to the ball. He grabbed it! Back to the basket it went. And right through the hoop! Wilkes had tied the game at 92–92.

In the next minute, Elvin Hayes was fouled. He made one of his free throws. The Bullets inched back in front 93–92.

There was just 1:45 left on the clock. Butch Beard took the ball for Golden State. He swung around Washington's Kevin Porter. He plunged down the side of the key. Wes Unseld loomed in front of him. Butch swept to the side and drove past. He went airborne with a perfect layup. Once again, the Warriors surged to the front — 94–93.

The fans were gasping. The impossible was happening. Golden State still had a chance for a clean sweep. The teams now traded the ball for several seconds. No one was able to score. But the pressure seemed to be getting to the Bullets.

Unseld sent a pass to Phil Chenier. The throw was bad, and the ball shot out of bounds. Then Dick Gibbs tried a layup. He missed. Finally, with just 29 seconds left, a Bullet fouled Butch Beard. Two free throws went to Butch. He made the first and missed the second. The score moved to 95–93 for the Warriors.

There was still time for the Bullets to tie things. They drove down under Golden State's basket. Phil Chenier risked a shot. The ball hit the backboard. It bounced high. Butch Beard jumped for the rebound. He was fouled by Elvin Hayes.

The foul gave Butch three chances to score 2 points. He could put the game out of Washington's reach.

He took his place in the free-throw circle. The

arena went quiet. The Washington fans cheered wildly when Butch missed his first two tries. But the third one dropped in. The Warriors' edge was up to 3 points — 96–93. Would it be enough for the win and the clean sweep?

It was! In the very last seconds, Wes Unseld tipped the ball in. The shot brought things to 96–95. But that was as far as the scoring was to go. The final buzzer sounded.

The team with only one superstar had the NBA crown. And they had the third clean sweep in the history of the league.

The Warriors knew that they had played a fine team game. Their teamwork had brought them from behind. It had enabled Rick Barry to take high scoring honors for the night with 20 points. It had helped Butch Beard to score 16 and Wilkes 12. And it had given them the finals in the best way possible — without a single loss.

Golden State Warrior
Rick Barry in action
against the Bullets'
Mike Riordan during
the 1974–75 playoffs.

The Bullets were a disappointed squad when they left the floor. They had won the NBA title (1948) while in Baltimore. But they had yet to bring the crown home to their new hometown. It came to them four years later. At the end of the 1978–79 season, they met Seattle in the finals. They downed the Super Sonics 4–3.

CHAPTER 6

TRIPLE OVERTIME

The NBA continued to grow as the 1970s passed. In 1974, the New Orleans Jazz joined the league. The number of teams was now up to eighteen.

Then, in 1975, four more teams joined. They were the Denver Nuggets, the Indiana Pacers, the New York Nets, and the San Antonio Spurs. They came from the rival American Basketball Association. The ABA had just gone out of business. It had been formed back in 1967 and had lasted for nine years.

The 1970s brought some other changes. The Washington Bullets were shifted from the Central Division to the Atlantic Division. The Detroit Pistons were also moved. They went from the Midwest Division to the Central.

Two teams changed cities. The Buffalo Braves went to San Diego. They became the Clippers of the Pacific Division. The Nets left New York City. Their new name was the New Jersey Nets.

By 1978, the NBA looked like this:

EASTERN CONFERENCE   WESTERN CONFERENCE

Atlantic Division
Boston Celtics
New Jersey Nets
New York Knickerbockers
Philadelphia 76ers
Washington Bullets

Midwest Division
Chicago Bulls
Denver Nuggets
Indiana Pacers
Kansas City Kings
Milwaukee Bucks

Central Division

Atlanta Hawks
Cleveland Cavaliers
Detroit Pistons
Houston Rockets
New Orleans Jazz
San Antonio Spurs

Pacific Division

Golden State Warriors
Los Angeles Lakers
Phoenix Suns
Portland Trail Blazers
San Diego Clippers
Seattle Super Sonics

The 1970s also saw some great moments in the playoffs. One of the greatest came in game 5 of the 1975–76 finals. The game went through three overtime periods. It was the first triple overtime in championship play.

1975–76
BOSTON CELTICS
vs.
PHOENIX SUNS

The finals stood tied at 2 apiece when game 5 opened. The Celtics had come to the finals after defeating Buffalo and Cleveland. The Suns beat Seattle and Golden State to get there.

Game 5 was played before 15,320 fans at Boston Garden. The teams battled to a 95–95 tie in regulation play. They fought even harder in the first overtime period. Each managed to score just 6 points. The score stood at 101–101.

The battle raged on through the second overtime. With less than a minute left, the score was locked at 106–106. Then the Celtics jumped to a 3-point lead.

But Tom Van Arsdale of the Suns quickly scored. Boston's edge was cut to 109–108. Next, Paul Westphal stole the ball from Boston's John Havlicek. Paul fired to Curtis Perry. Curtis tried a 15-foot (4.6-m) toss. The ball hit the rim. It flew back to Curtis. He grabbed it and let loose with a jumper. This time, the ball sailed through the hoop. The Suns were an inch ahead — 110–109.

Seconds later, Havlicek took the ball for Boston. The clock was almost out. He drove past Ricky Sobers. John didn't break stride as he flew into the air. The ball went arcing toward the basket 15 feet (4.6 m) away. It brushed the backboard — and dropped through the hoop.

The Boston fans went wild. Their team had a 111–110 victory — and the crown. Hundreds of spectators poured out onto the floor. They were a rowdy lot. They began pushing their way through the players and the officials.

Suddenly, there was trouble. Phoenix players tried to protect themselves from being roughed up. Fistfights broke out. One fan grabbed referee Richie Powers and began to wrestle with him. Someone else threw a courtside table over on its side. A basket support was almost torn down.

Security policemen rushed into the mess. They were hopelessly outnumbered. Ten minutes passed before the floor was clear again. And there was referee Powers standing with one arm upraised.

Boston's John Havlicek
dribbles his way to a basket
in the 1975–76 finals.

He was signaling that the game *hadn't* ended on Havlicek's throw. There were 2 seconds left!

The Suns were to take a throw-in at the endline. They knew one thing for sure. They didn't have time to get clear down the court and make a basket. To have any chance at all, they had to take the throw-in at midcourt.

And so the Suns pulled a trick that would move them to midcourt. They had already taken all their time-outs. But they called for another. It was an illegal request. With the clock stopped, the ball was handed to Boston for a free throw. Jo Jo White sank the shot. The score moved to 112–110.

But the Suns had gotten the throw-in at midcourt — and the chance to tie things. They went to work fast. They fired the ball to Garfield Heard. He jumped high and sailed a shot to the basket. The ball dropped through the hoop on the buzzer.

The plan had worked. The Suns had saved themselves. Maybe they could win in the third overtime.

The fans were wilder than ever as play continued. They kept dashing onto the court and interfering with the players. Cups, waste paper — and even a couple of tennis balls — rained down from the balconies. Play was slowed almost to a crawl.

Yet the Celtics managed to run up a 6-point lead. There were just 36 seconds left. The Suns cut that lead to 2 points by quickly scoring twice. But then Jo Jo White took over for Boston. He dribbled out the last seconds. The win went to Boston 128–126.

Boston now held a 3–2 edge in the series. They went on to win game 6 by a 7-point margin — 87–80. They had their thirteenth NBA crown.

1976–77
PORTLAND TRAIL BLAZERS
vs.
PHILADELPHIA 76ers

This was the "comeback series" for the Portland Trail Blazers. That's what the sportswriters called it.

Led by center Bill Walton, the Blazers looked good early in the playoffs. They beat Chicago, Denver, and Los Angeles.

But they sure didn't look like winners in the championship round. The Philadelphia 76ers had plowed over Boston and Houston to reach the finals. Now the Blazers lost games 1 and 2 to them.

The fans said Philadelphia would take the

crown. The Blazers were done. No team in NBA history had ever come from 2 games behind to win the finals.

But Portland surprised them. The Blazers started along the comeback trail by taking the next two games. Then they nailed down game 5. They now led the series 3–2.

The fans wondered if a miracle might be in the works when game 6 began. Portland surged to a 67–55 lead by halftime. The Blazers were still ahead — 91–82 — when the final period opened.

When there were just 6 minutes left, they held a 12-point edge. Bill Walton was playing one of the greatest games of his career. By the final buzzer, he would score 20 points and make 23 rebounds and 7 assists. Bob Gross would be high man for Portland with 24 points.

But Philadelphia wasn't ready to give up yet. Fighting hard, the 76ers closed to within 4 points.

Bill Walton (dark uniform)
of the Portland Trail Blazers
in action against Philadelphia's
Caldwell Jones during the
1976–77 finals.

Then they picked up another point on a free throw. The Blazers pulled away with a 2-pointer. The 76ers came back with two more free throws. Finally, with just 18 seconds left to go, George McGinnis gave Philadelphia a basket. The scoreboard read 109–107 for the Blazers.

The Portland fans held their breath. The 76ers forced a jump ball. They took possession. They now tried to score three times. Their top players — Julius Erving, Lloyd Free, and George McGinnis — all sent the ball to the basket. Three shots — and three misses!

The miracle had happened. The Blazers still held a 109–107 lead when the buzzer sounded.

They owned their first NBA crown. Bill Walton and his teammates had staged the greatest comeback in the league's history.

The Blazers started something with their comeback. In the 1978-79 finals, the Seattle Super Sonics decided to imitate them. They lost game 1 to the Washington Bullets. Then they caught fire. They won the next four games in a row to take the title.

The Sonics and the Bullets had met in the 1977-78 finals. Washington won that series 3–2, taking the NBA crown to its new hometown for the first time.

CHAPTER
7

INTO
THE '80s

The 1980s opened with another big win for Los Angeles. The Lakers wrapped up the 1979-80 season by beating the Philadelphia 76ers for the crown. The Lakers took the finals 4–2.

That championship series saw brilliant play by two Lakers. They were the veteran Kareem Abdul-Jabbar and the rookie Earvin "Magic" Johnson.

Kareem led the team for the first 5 games. He averaged 33.4 points, 13.6 rebounds, and 4.6 blocked shots. He was performing at his best. But then he was injured in game 5. His face full of pain, Kareem was helped from the court. He was out of the series with a sprained ankle.

The Lakers went on to win the game 108–103. But the L.A. fans were worried. What would their team do without its top player? They needn't have worried. Johnson took over in game 6. He lived up to his nickname, "Magic."

Just look at what he did. Magic played at three positions — center, forward, and guard. He scored 42 points. He made 5 rebounds. And he grabbed 3 steals.

His shooting was especially good from the field. Magic hit 12 field goals in the first half. He followed with 7 out of 11 in the next two quarters.

And his free throws were even better. Johnson took 14. He made them all.

Thanks to Magic — and to fine play by his teammates — the Lakers swept to a 123–107 victory. It gave them their seventh NBA crown, and their second for Los Angeles. They had won five many years ago as the Minneapolis Lakers.

And so the 1980s opened with a fine championship series. Another one followed.

Earvin "Magic" Johnson
took over for the
Los Angeles Lakers when
Kareem Abdul-Jabbar was
injured in game 5 of the
1979–80 finals. In game 6
"Magic" scored 42 points
against the tough 76ers.

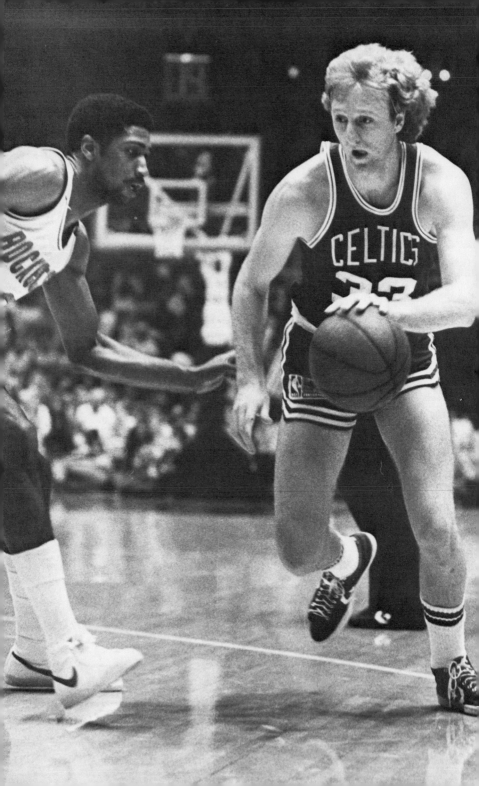

1980–81
BOSTON CELTICS
vs.
HOUSTON ROCKETS

The Celts were in the finals again. They had posted a solid 60–22 season. Then they had knocked off the 76ers in the semifinals. Now they faced a strong Houston squad for the crown.

The Rockets had begun life in 1967 at San Diego. They moved to Houston in 1971. This was their first championship series. They were led by 6-foot 10-inch (2.08-m) Moses Malone. Moses had first played as a pro in the ABA, back in 1974. He came to the Rockets two years later. So far in his career, Moses had scored more than 6,400 points. He had become the game's top rebounder.

The Rockets were strong. But many sportswriters favored Boston for a quick win. In the first games, it seemed as if the Celts believed them. Maybe they expected an easy time. They sure

Boston's Larry Bird
charges along the court
in the 1980–81 battle
with the Houston Rockets.

didn't perform at their best. But Houston did. The result: the series was soon tied at 2–2.

Then something remarkable happened. Moses Malone was a quiet man. But now he spoke up. He told reporters that the Celts weren't "all that good." Moses added that, with "four guys off the street" from his hometown, he could beat the Celts.

Moses' remarks landed on the sports pages everywhere. One Boston paper printed his remarks in extra-heavy black type. Bill Fitch, the Celtic coach, cut the words out of the paper. He pasted them to every locker in the team's dressing room. No player would be allowed to forget them.

From then on, Houston was in trouble. The Celts were angry. They let loose with a fast-break offense in game 5. Houston took a 109–80 thumping. They fell behind 3–2 in the series.

The top Boston man in the game was forward Cedric Maxwell. Working against Moses Malone, he scored 24 points and took 15 rebounds.

Boston was still angry in game 6. For a time, the Celts put up with a 12–12 tie. Then they burst into the lead. At halftime, they led 53–47. They pushed ahead to 82–67 in the third period. The lead was so big because the Celts hit 13 of 18 shots in the second and third frames. Their shooting average stood at a high 72 percent. Houston managed to sink only 41 percent of its shots in the entire game.

Boston moved the score to 84–67 in the fourth quarter. But then either the Celts let down or Houston caught fire. The Rockets went on a scoring streak. They dropped in 11 straight points. It was all done in just under 4 minutes. The score closed to 84–78.

At the same time, the Rockets threw a pressure defense at Boston. It caused the Celts to miss 6 shots in a row. It also forced them into a turnover. Coach Bill Fitch watched from the sidelines. He turned pale with anger.

Boston finally managed a basket. But Houston still came on hard. The score moved to 86–83. Just a few moments ago, the Rockets had been 17 points behind. Now they were nipping at Boston's heels. About 4 minutes remained on the clock.

Then all eyes went to Boston forward Larry Bird. He had the ball at the baseline near the left corner. Rocket Calvin Garrett was guarding him. Larry jumped high. The ball sailed to the basket 15 feet (4.6 m) away. And Boston's lead jumped to 88–83.

Larry had been having a strange series. He'd been great in one way and poor in another. He'd done fine on rebounds, making about 16 per game.

And he led both teams in assists and steals. But he'd been in a terrible scoring slump. He'd averaged only 13 points in the first 5 games.

But now the slump came to an end. In the last 4 minutes, Larry took the Celts to victory.

Right after his shot from the baseline, Larry was fouled. He dropped in a free throw, moving the score to 89–83. The Rockets inched to 89–87 with free throws of their own. As soon as he had the ball again, Larry lobbed a pass over Moses Malone's head. Cedric Maxwell made the reception. He scooted under the basket for a perfect layup. The score: 91–87.

In the next seconds, the score changed to 92–87. Then Larry had the ball again. He dribbled to the left corner. The basket loomed 24 feet (7.3 m) away. He let the ball fly. If it dropped in, Larry would have a 3-pointer. . . .

It did.

At that moment, there was just 1:36 left to play. Sportswriters later said that Larry's shot broke Houston's back. In that final 1:36, Boston ran its total to 102. The Rockets got only as far as 91.

And it was all over for 1980-81.

The Celtics had won their first NBA crown in the 1956-57 playoffs. They had been big winners throughout the 1960s. They had taken two championships in the 1970s. Now they had started the 1980s in the best way possible — with their fourteenth title.

They were the "winningest" team in pro basketball. Will they take even more crowns? Only time will tell.

All the teams that have played in the championship rounds have been big winners, whether they took the NBA crown or not.

They've all given us great players — from George Mikan, Bob Cousy, and Walt Frazier to Elgin Baylor, Bill Russell, Wilt Chamberlain, Jerry West, Bill Walton, and today's Magic Johnson.

And they've given us great moments of court action — from the Celts' triple overtime to the Blazers' sensational 4-game comeback.

Who was the greatest of the players? And what single moment of action was the greatest of all? No one can say.

But one thing *can* be said. Future NBA playoffs will bring us more great players and more great moments. You can count on it.

THE NBA CHAMPIONSHIPS

THE RESULTS

1949-50

Minneapolis	4
Syracuse	2

1950-51

Rochester	4
New York	3

1951-52

Minneapolis	4
New York	3

1952-53

Minneapolis	4
New York	1

1953-54

Minneapolis	4
Syracuse	3

1954-55

Syracuse	4
Fort Wayne	3

1955-56

Philadelphia	4
Fort Wayne	1

1956-57

Boston	4
St. Louis	3

1957-58

St. Louis	4
Boston	2

1958-59

Boston	4
Minneapolis	0

1959-60

Boston	4
St. Louis	3

1960-61

Boston	4
St. Louis	1

1961-62		1971-72	
Boston	4	Los Angeles	4
Los Angeles	3	New York	1

1962-63		1972-73	
Boston	4	New York	4
Los Angeles	2	Los Angeles	1

1963-64		1973-74	
Boston	4	Boston	4
San Francisco	1	Milwaukee	3

1964-65		1974-75	
Boston	4	Golden State	4
Los Angeles	1	Washington	0

1965-66		1975-76	
Boston	4	Boston	4
Los Angeles	3	Phoenix	2

1966-67		1976-77	
Philadelphia	4	Portland	4
San Francisco	2	Philadelphia	2

1967-68		1977-78	
Boston	4	Washington	4
Los Angeles	2	Seattle	3

1968-69		1978-79	
Boston	4	Seattle	4
Los Angeles	3	Washington	1

1969-70		1979-80	
New York	4	Los Angeles	4
Los Angeles	3	Philadelphia	2

1970-71		1980-81	
Milwaukee	4	Boston	4
Baltimore	0	Houston	2

INDEX

WATERLOO HIGH SCHOOL LIBRARY
1464 INDUSTRY RD.
ATWATER, OHIO 44201

The NBA Championships   11714
Dolan, Edward
                                         796.32 Dol